FAT-FIGHTING FRUIT

A compound called (–)-hydroxycitric acid (HCA) has been discovered in an exotic fruit that not only gives you more energy while lessening the appetite, it also helps prevent the carbohydrates you consume (in starches, fruits, vegetables and sugars) from being converted into fat. This is the first natural weight-loss compound which accomplishes this without adversely affecting the central nervous system and causing side effects such as anxiety or the jitters. The latest research and information on this fascinating discovery—and what it could mean for your health—is both summarized for laypeople and explained in detail for health professionals within.

ABOUT THE AUTHORS

Dallas Clouatre received his Ph.D. from the University of California at Berkeley in 1990, and his academic interests continue in the history of philosophy, the philosophy of science and comparative medical systems. He has taught at his alma mater and the University of San Francisco, and his book, *Anti-Fat Nutrients* (PAX Publishing) is now in its second edition. Dr. Clouatre's articles have appeared in *Critical Review,* the *Journal of the History of Ideas* and the *California Chiropractic Association Journal.* He also acts as a consultant for vitamin and cosmetic companies in the U.S., and herbal product manufacturers throughout Asia.

Michael Rosenbaum studied at New York City's Albert Einstein College of Medicine in 1968 and trained as a resident in psychiatry at the University of California School of Medicine in San Francisco. His articles on preventive medicine and health have appeared in *Medical World News, Let's Live, Healthworld* and *The Townsend Letter for Doctors.* He is the author of *SuperSupplements* (Viking-Penguin) and *Chlorella* (Keats Publishing, Inc.), and the co-author of *Solving the Puzzle of Chronic Fatigue Syndrome* (Life Science Press). Dr. Rosenbaum practices preventive medicine, clinical nutrition, allergy and immunology in Marin County and Santa Monica, California.

The Diet and Health Benefits of HCA (Hydroxycitric Acid) is not intended as medical advice. Its intent is solely informational and educational. Please consult a health professional should the need for one be indicated.

THE DIET AND HEALTH BENEFITS OF HCA (HYDROXYCITRIC ACID)

ISBN: 0-87983-656-3

Printed in the United States of America

Good Health Guides are published by
Keats Publishing, Inc.
27 Pine Street, Box 876
New Canaan, Connecticut 06840-0876

THE DIET AND HEALTH BENEFITS OF HCA

(HYDROXYCITRIC ACID)

HOW THIS ALL-NATURAL DIET AID PROMOTES WEIGHT LOSS AND INHIBITS FAT PRODUCTION

---

by Dallas Clouatre, Ph.D.
and Michael Rosenbaum, M.D.

Keats Publishing, Inc. New Canaan, Connecticut

CONTENTS

INTRODUCTION

Estimates by the U.S. Public Health Service and other agencies which collect health statistics indicate that obesity is causally associated with 300,000 or more deaths each year. This figure dwarfs the death toll from AIDS and other highly publicized sources of mortality, and yet even this number may be too small. Excess weight either causes or exacerbates an array of health and social problems. On the health front, these range from cardiovascular disease and stroke through diabetes and hyperlipidemia, to osteoarthritis and infertility. Social and psychological problems related to excess weight include increased risks of injury at work and at home, reduced mobility and ability to participate in activities, loss of income and depression.[1] Moreover, there are other health syndromes, such as Syndrome X, which are related to problems in weight control even though excess weight may not be immediately at issue. Safe, natural products which offer solutions for effective weight control and related metabolic problems—including cholesterol and other blood lipid problems—therefore can be of great benefit. One such product may well be the Indian fruit extract known by the formidable chemical names *(–)-hydroxycitrate* and *(–)-hydroxycitric acid*. For the sake of simplicity, in this booklet the extract will be called HCA.

HCA, which chemically is very similar to the citric acid found in oranges and other citrus fruits, is extracted from the dried fruit rind of several South Asian trees of the genus *Garcinia*. The highest concentration of HCA is found in the species *Garcinia cambogia*. Long favored as a souring agent for pork and fish dishes in the coastal areas of southern India, the crude extract of this fruit traditionally has been used to

Garcinia cambogia fruit

improve digestion and to make meals more satisfying. Extracts of the rind also are used medicinally in South Asia, including in the treatment of angina. Unlike citric acid, which is found in many plants, hydroxycitric acid in the particular (–) chemical form (referring to the manner in which the molecule is structured) is extremely rare in nature. Specialists in plant compounds became aware of the remarkable qualities of HCA only in the late 1960s, at which point they began to learn that this not-quite citric acid compound can reduce the body's production of fats from carbohydrates. This startling finding prompted the pharmaceutical giant Hoffmann-La Roche in 1970 to begin to investigate the physiological effects of HCA. These studies continued for many years, and the patents which they generated were still being accepted as late as 1984. Other laboratories remain active in the field of HCA research. The information in this booklet comes from the dozens of papers published on HCA which have appeared over a period of three decades of active research.

The intensive research conducted on HCA over the last several decades indicates something about the promise which this compound holds with regard to various health issues. Investigators have been particularly interested in the following areas, which involve weight control, the modulation of blood lipid levels and energy metabolism:

- The conversion of carbohydrates to fats—HCA reduces the rate of conversion of dietary carbohydrate calories to fat, i.e., it inhibits lipogenesis
- The production of low-density lipoprotein (LDL) and triglycerides—HCA may lower the production of both cholesterol and fatty acids as a result of its effects upon metabolism
- Energy levels and glycogen storage—experimental evidence shows that HCA increases the production of glycogen in the liver (and probably in peripheral tissues), which promises greater and more sustained energy for those with glycogen storage problems
- Appetite control—both preclinical and clinical evidence indicate that HCA suppresses appetite and thereby reduces food intake, although exact dosage levels remain to be established
- Thermogenesis—some authors speculate that HCA may increase the body's production of heat (and thus the burning of calories) in response to food consumption by activating the process of thermogenesis.[2]

HCA is safe to use. It is a naturally occurring compound which is as safe, perhaps safer, than is the citric acid found in orange juice and which is used extensively in commercial food production. HCA has a further advantage over many other weight-loss products in that *it does not act upon the central nervous system.* This means that it is not a stimulant, that it will not interfere with sleep and that it will not cause changes in heart rate or blood pressure. The Hoffmann-La Roche laboratory studies showed no side effects at the dosages which suppressed appetite, and the limited preliminary human studies which have been conducted in South Carolina and at the University of Arizona indicated no adverse effects.

HCA has shown itself to be extremely effective in laboratory experiments, and it has proven useful as a diet aid in two recent U.S. human clinical trials. Currently, work is being directed toward providing better answers to a number of related questions, such as the following:

1. What dosage provides the best weight-loss results? Extrapolations from animal studies indicate that effective dosages range from 3-6 grams per day, yet trial human studies suggest that roughly 750 mg of HCA per day has an appreciable effect when taken in conjunction with the proper adjunctive supplements.
2. We know that HCA should be administered more than once per day, but what dosage schedule leads to maximum results?
3. What range of other nutrients, herbs or supplements should be taken along with HCA to increase its impact upon appetite, fat storage and glycogen production?
4. Is it necessary to modify the everyday diet in order to take full advantage of the benefits of HCA?

This booklet provides an overview of the history of research into the effects of HCA. It explains the science behind the product, the benefits which can be expected, and considerations which should be taken into account when buying a commercial source of HCA.

WHAT IS *GARCINIA CAMBOGIA*?

THE BOTANY OF A NATURAL PRODUCT

Garcinia cambogia is one of several closely related *Garcinia* species from the plant family known as Guttiferae. With thin skin and deep vertical lobes, the fruit of *G. cambogia* is about the size of an orange, but it looks more like a small yellowish or sometimes reddish pumpkin. (The color can vary considerably.) When the rinds are dried and cured in preparation for storage and extraction, they are dark brown in color. Another member of the family, *G. mangostana* (or *G. mangostienia*), is cultivated specifically for its fruit and is not a source of HCA. Species other than *G. cambogia* with significant HCA content and which sometimes are used interchangeably with *G. cambogia* in food preparation are *G. atroviridis* and *G. indica*. These *Garcinia* species are native to Southeast Asia and usually are wild-crafted, but they also are cultivated in some areas. The organic acid known as (–)-hydroxycitric acid, i.e., HCA, is the primary acid found in the fruit and the rinds of *G. cambogia, G. atroviridis* and *G. indica*. The highest concentration of HCA is found in the first of these. In *G. cambogia*, from 10 to (rarely) 30 percent of the weight of the dried pericarp (rind) is HCA. The acid occurs in nature almost entirely in the form of its lactone, which has a chemical structure and physiologic effects which are different from those of the free acid.[3]

Along the west coast of South India, *G. cambogia* is popularly termed "Malabar Tamarind," which is actually a quite different species (*Tamarindis indica*). The latter is a small and the former a quite large evergreen tree. The two have the same culinary uses.[4] *G. cambogia* is also called "Goraka" or, in some areas, simply "Kattcha puli" (souring fruit). *G. cambogia* is employed commercially in fish curing, especially in Sri Lanka (Colombo curing), and various species of *Garcinia* are used similarly in food preparation in Thailand, Malaysia, Burma and other Southeast Asian countries.

G. cambogia is used primarily in cooking, including in the preparation of curries. The fruit rind and extracts of *Garcinia* species are called for in many traditional recipes. In the Indian Ayurvedic healing system, "sour" flavors are said to activate digestion. In the areas in which it is consumed, *G. cambogia* is considered to be effective in making meals more "filling."[5] The "Colombo curing" of fish is a commercial enterprise of fish preservation typical of South India which makes use of the antibacterial qualities of the acid. ("Colombo curing" is especially associated with the island nation of Sir Lanka, formerly Ceylon.) Aside from its use in food preparation and preservation, extracts of *G. cambogia* are sometimes used as purgatives in the treatment of intestinal worms and other parasites, for tumors, for dysentery and in the treatment of bilious digestive conditions. Less commonly, extracts are employed as cardiotonics to treat angina.[6]

Neither acute nor chronic toxicity is reported with the regular consumption of *Garcinia* products as either food or tonics. These products have been used routinely throughout the coastal areas of South Asia for centuries, and they continue to be consumed in copious amounts as both foods and tonics today.

THREE DECADES OF RESEARCH

Although HCA is only beginning to become widely known in the health food industry in 1994, research on HCA stretches back more than thirty years. First identified in the late nineteenth century, hydroxycitric acid did not become the topic of sustained interest until after the publication in 1964 and 1965 of the studies of Y. S. Lewis and S. Neelakantan of the Central Food Technology Research Institute of Mysore, India.[7] These researchers identified the most important plant sources of hydroxycitrate in its (–) form and provided early data on the characteristics of the lactone, which is the reconfigured molecule of the acid formed as water is excluded from its structure. At this point, it was still a matter of speculation as to the precise role which this and related acids played in plant physiology. In 1969 Y. S. Lewis published a further article on hydroxycitric acid which clarified the four isomers (molecular configurations) possible and identified the chemical structures of the corresponding lactones for two of these. In the same year, the absolute configurations of the hydroxycitric acids and their lactones were established by the University of Copenhagen chemists Per M. Boll, Else Sørensen and Erik Balieu and verified in a personal communication between Lewis and the Danish scientists.[8]

Again in 1969, researchers at the Graduate Department of Biochemistry at Brandeis University who were doing work on the Krebs/Citric Acid Cycle—which is the basic energy cycle of the body—began studies of the role of (–)-hydroxycitrate as an inhibitor in one of the steps of this cycle. They discovered that HCA prevented the activity of the important enzyme *ATP-citrate lyase* (which is central to the process of lipogenesis as discussed below).[9] The key figure in this early research was John M. Lowenstein, who over the next several years, either alone or with co-authors, published a number of studies on HCA and its special properties.[10] It was Dr. Lowenstein who brought HCA to the attention of the pharmaceutical giant Hoffmann-La Roche and who wrote the first of a long series of U.S. patents granted to Hoffmann-La Roche for the use of HCA and related compounds in the treatment of obesity.[11] (This was primarily a use patent. Compounds which are naturally occurring *per se* cannot be patented.)

At Hoffmann-La Roche the emphasis of research shifted from the elucidation of the basic biochemical mechanisms of HCA's effects to the search for its impact upon the physiological sources of obesity and the overproduction of blood lipids. Here the chief researchers over the years were Ann C. Sullivan and Joseph Triscari. Much of their work clarified the ways in which HCA affects various tissues in the body. Inasmuch as HCA itself is a naturally occurring substance, the chief interest of the pharmaceutical research was to use HCA as a prototype for the development of related synthetic compounds which would be patentable.

THE CHEMISTRY OF HCA

Hydroxycitric acid is known to have four isomers, which is to say that the molecule of the acid with the same number of carbon, hydrogen and oxygen atoms can be arranged in four different shapes, each with slightly different effects upon the body. The *Garcinia* species already discussed contain the form called (–)-

erythro-L_S-hydroxycitric acid. Some other plants, such as *Hibiscus sabdariffa*, contain the isomer (+)-*threo*-L_S-hydroxycitric acid, which is also called (+)-*allo*-L_S-hydroxycitric acid. (The exact chemical names can vary with the scientific convention employed.) Both of these acids are found in nature in the form of their lactones. Their configurations are shown in Figure 1.

The significance of the chemistry, as will be explained shortly, is that only the extract from the *Garcinia* species actively prevents the body from changing carbohydrate calories into fats. Moreover, the researchers at both Brandeis University and at Hoffmann-La Roche very early in their studies concluded that only the acid form of (–)-hydroxycitrate and the various salts of HCA can inhibit fat formation. The lactone proved ineffective for this purpose.

HCA works by fooling the body into thinking that it (HCA) is its own close chemical cousin, citrate. To accomplish this task, HCA must be in a form which closely resembles the form in which citrate is actually found in the cells. If the lactone of HCA is consumed, it must be returned to its acid form by the reincorporation of a molecule of water through a process called "hydrolysis" before it becomes active. Exposure of the lactone to a chemical "base" is necessary for this process. As of this writing, there are no published studies which indicate that this hydrolysis takes place with any degree of efficiency in the body. (See "Choosing the Right Product.") In Figure 1 it can be seen that the lactone has lost 2 hydrogen (H) atoms and 1 oxygen (O) atom, and as a result a bond not originally present has formed between two ends of the HCA molecule. This produces a "ring" structure. (See Figure 1.)

HOW HCA WORKS

Each of the next several sections provides a biochemical and/or a physiological explanation for the actions of HCA and then the experimental evidence which supports each explanation. Since these explanations can be somewhat technical for those who are not trained in the sciences, **a summary in bold-faced type precedes the more difficult sections** to provide the average reader (or the reader in a hurry) with a description of what is being explained.

In a nutshell, HCA acts as a "partitioning agent" in the metabo-

Figure 1. The Chemical Configurations of Two Hydroxycitrates and Lactone[12]

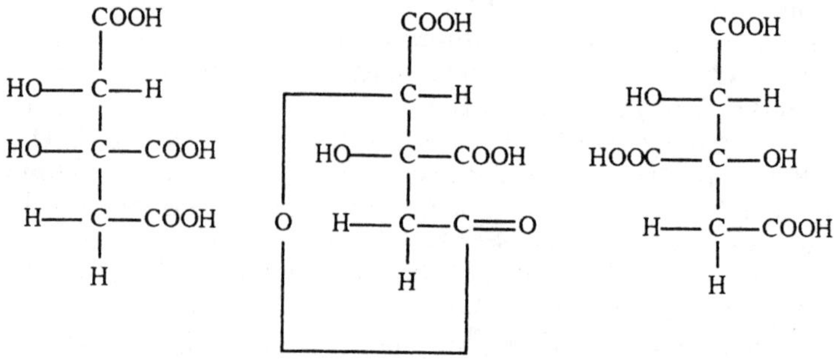

```
        COOH                    COOH                    COOH
         |                       |                       |
   HO—— C——H           ———————  C——H           HO——    C——H
         |             |         |                       |
   HO—— C——COOH        |  HO—— C——COOH       HOOC——    C——OH
         |             |         |                       |
    H—— C——COOH        O   H—— C——C==O          H——    C——COOH
         |             |         |     |                 |
         H             |         H     |                 H
                       |_______________|
```

(–) -*erythro*-hydroxy citric acid from Garcinia spp.

(–) -*erythro*-hydroxy citric acid lactone

(+) -*allo*-hydroxy citric acid from Hibiscus sabdariffa

lism of carbohydrates. During the normal metabolism of meals, carbohydrate calories, if these are not immediately used for energy nor stored as glycogen, are converted to fats. This conversion takes place both in peripheral tissues and, most importantly, in the liver. HCA serves to divert calories away from fat production and toward the production of glycogen, the special energy storage starch (more accurately, a polysaccharide) found in the liver and in the muscles.

The actual conversion of excess carbohydrate into fats is performed in several steps. Two of these are especially important for our discussion. First, a small energy molecule derived from glucose called pyruvate (or pyruvic acid) is broken into yet smaller acetyl units within the mitochondria, the energy factories of the cells. These smaller units are then moved outside of the mitochondria to the cytosol, the protoplasm of the cell, in the form of citrate (citric acid) and transformed into fatty acids and cholesterol. *The enzyme responsible for this transformation is ATP-citrate lyase,* the citrate "cleavage" enzyme.

HCA interferes with the functioning of this enzyme by imitating the chemical structure of the citrate produced in the Krebs Cycle (also called the Citric Acid Cycle). HCA binds the cleavage enzyme before it can release acetyl units from the citrate which has entered the cytosol of the cell (the fluid portion of the cellular cytoplasm). In so doing, it not only blocks the production of fats, but it also reduces the appetite, uses up a significant amount of energy and, perhaps, stimulates thermogenesis. The pattern for the following discussions is laid out in Figure 2.

BLOCKING THE ENZYME ATP-CITRATE LYASE

Summary

HCA reduces the conversion of carbohydrate calories into fats. It does this by inhibiting the actions of ATP-citrate lyase, the enzyme which converts citrate into fatty acids and cholesterol in the primary pathway of fat synthesis in the body. The actions of HCA increase the production and storage of glycogen (which is found in the liver, small intestine and muscles) while reducing both appetite and weight gain. HCA also causes calories to be burned in an energy cycle similar to thermogenesis.

The enzyme ATP-citrate lyase is important as part of one of the earliest steps of the Krebs Cycle metabolic pathway. As carbohydrates are broken down for energy, pyruvic acid is formed and combined with coenzyme A or CoA (a compound containing vitamin B5) to produce acetyl-CoA. For each molecule of the simple sugar glucose which goes through the cycle, two acetyl-CoA molecules are created, and each of these forms a molecule of the high-energy compound ATP (adenosine triphosphate). ATP is the form of energy which is immediately available to the muscles and for use in biosynthetic activities.

When carbohydrate calories as pyruvate enter the Krebs Cycle at a rate which exceeds the body's immediate needs for energy, the excess calories are removed from the Cycle at an early stage. The 6-carbon molecule of glucose is first broken down into the 3-carbon

Figure 2. The Krebs/Citric Acid Cycle in Fatty Acid Synthesis from Glucose

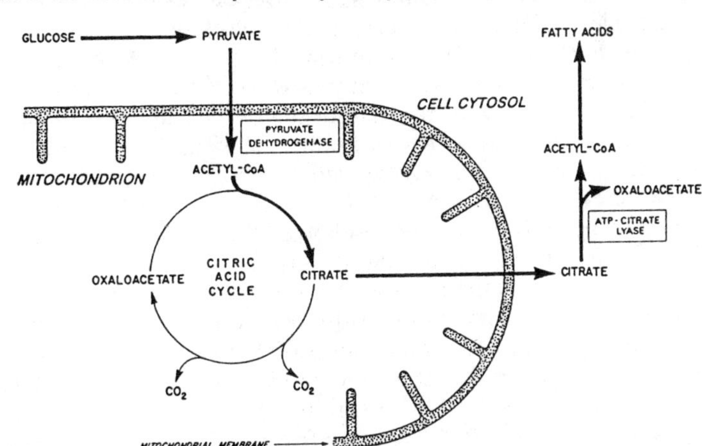

pyruvate and then this pyruvate itself is broken to create 2-carbon molecules called acetates (think of the acid found in vinegar). This last step is the source of acetyl-CoA. If for some reason this early step works at a rate faster than the rest of the cycle, such as when energy requirements are low, then the acetyl-CoA is removed from the mitochondrion and turned into either fatty acids or cholesterol.

The process of creating acetyl-CoA takes place entirely *inside* the mitochondria of the cells, but it happens that acetyl-CoA cannot pass through the membrane of the mitochondria. Moreover, the production of fatty acids and cholesterol takes place entirely *outside* of the mitochondria in the cytosol of the cell. Citrate provides a solution to this problem: the acetyl group is removed from the mitochondrion as citrate, which can pass through the membrane. Once across the mitochondrial membrane, citrate is "cleaved" by the enzyme ATP-citrate lyase to release the acetyl group. The acetyl group then is converted into fat.

HCA, which might be called an "impersonator" of citrate, works by acting as a competitive inhibitor of the enzyme ATP-citrate lyase within the following reaction pathway of fatty acid biosynthesis in the presence of the divalent ion of magnesium:

ATP + citrate + CoA → acetyl-CoA + oxaloacetate + ADP + P_i
[in the mitochondrion] [outside the mitochondrion in the cytosol]

where ATP = adenosine triphosphate, CoA = coenzyme A, ADP = adenosine diphosphate and P_i = orthophosphate ion. Citrate is synthesized from oxaloacetate and acetate. *Since HCA does not itself readily penetrate the mitochondrion, the compound does not influence the oxidative decarboxylation of pyruvate, oxidative phosphorylation, respiration, or energy production in the Krebs Cycle.*[13]

The effectiveness of HCA both as an inhibitor of ATP-citrate lyase and as an influence upon appetite and weight gain depends upon several contingent factors. First, does HCA bind the enzyme permanently or only temporarily? The answer here is the latter; HCA is a potent inhibitor when it is present above certain concentrations in the cell, but it does not permanently bind the enzyme to itself. But the success of HCA in preventing the removal of acetyl-CoA from the mitochondrion to the cytosol of the cell where fat production takes place also depends upon there being no efficient alternate pathways for the acetyl groups to cross the mitochondrial membrane. As Figure 3 shows, there are, in fact, at least four known pathways. One of these, the direct movement of acetyl-CoA across the membrane, is almost totally inactive. A second, movement via citrate, can be largely blocked by HCA. How-

Figure 3. Possible Pathways of Acetyl-CoA Across the Mitochondrial Membrane

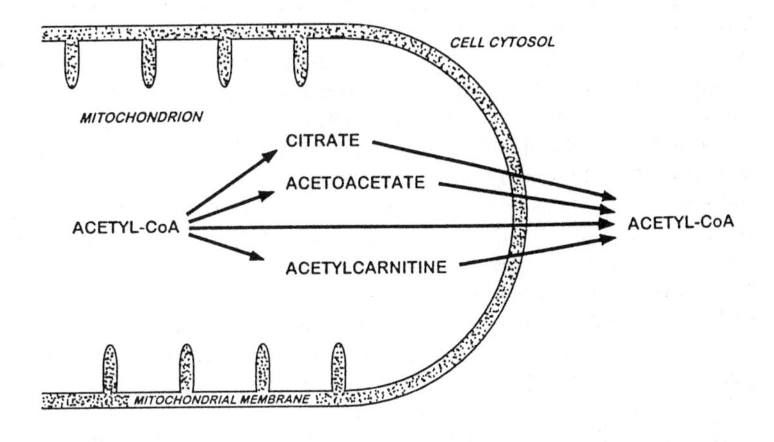

ever, two other pathways are potentially of importance. These are the movement of acetoacetate and the movement of acetylcarnitine across the membrane. Either of these pathways can substitute to some limited extent for the citrate pathway. Current research aims at discovering how effective these alternate pathways are and whether they become more significant under certain circumstances. In animal trials, neither has proved significant, but the activities of these pathways vary from species to species.[14]

What happens after HCA blocks the actions of ATP-citrate lyase? Our actual understanding at the biochemical level at this point is largely speculative, but it appears that glycolysis is slowed in its early steps and even reversed at some points so as to favor the production of glycogen over that of fat. HCA does not penetrate the mitochondria itself except at extremely high concentrations. Neither does it directly prevent citrate from forming and reaching the cytosol. However, by obstructing the cleavage actions of the ATP-citrate lyase enzyme, HCA causes an increase in the concentration of citrate in the cytosol, and this factor, in turn, reduces the transport of citrate across the mitochondrial membrane. A build-up of citrate within the mitochondrion then reduces the formation of new citrate by inhibiting the enzyme citrate synthase (which creates citrate out of oxaloacetate and acetyl units). This increases the amount of acetyl-CoA in the mitochondrion. There follows, in turn, a decrease in the splitting of pyruvate to produce acetyl units since the presence of large amounts of acetyl-CoA and/or the high-energy coenzyme NADH (nicotinamide adenine dinucleotide) inhibit the enzyme which splits pyruvate to yield new acetyl units for the Krebs Cycle. Large amounts of either citrate or ATP also strongly inhibit at an earlier stage the entire general pathway of glycolysis, the pathway which splits carbohydrates into glucose and then into pyruvate.

Returning to the Krebs Cycle itself, the increase in citrate inside the mitochondrion leads to an increase (transient?) in oxaloacetate within the cycle. Under these high-energy conditions, this oxaloacetate does not lead to the production of more citrate, but instead leads to the production of new glucose (gluconeogenesis) and thereby probably more glycogen.[15] Some acetyl groups will leave the mitochondrion by way of acetoacetate and acetylcarnitine, albeit to a limited extent. Other mechanisms may be involved as well. (See "Stimulating Thermogenesis?") Figure 4 shows the pertinent regulation and control mechanisms in the coordinated glycolytic and Krebs Cycle pathways.

Several consequences result from the foregoing: First, the metabolism of carbohydrates into pyruvate is radically slowed. This means that even before reactions reach the Krebs Cycle, there is strong pressure within the reaction pathway for carbohydrate calories to be stored as glycogen. At least three different points of regulation prevent glucose from being broken down into pyruvate. Second, the pyruvate which does reach the Krebs Cycle as acetyl-CoA is again blocked by excess citrate, and the cycle slows. Virtually all regulation of the energy flow would take place simply to prevent the formation of new citrate. The remaining citrate which could not leave the mitochondria at the first step in the Krebs Cycle to produce fatty acids and cholesterol continues through the cycle and ultimately is changed into oxaloacetate as the last product of the cycle. The increased amount of oxaloacetate found at the end of the cycle (oxaloacetate which now cannot be changed into citrate) is used to recreate glucose, the original source of pyruvate with which the Citric Acid Cycle began. This glucose would be carried back into the cytosol of the cell and some of it would end up stored as glycogen. The amount of actual gluconeogenesis which takes place probably is very small. In two human trials conducted by Dr. Anthony Conte, a bariatric physician in South Carolina, blood tests from his subjects who were using HCA revealed that although these subjects felt more energetic, blood sugar levels actually went down rather than up. This implies that gluconeogenesis is quite limited and that HCA is safe for diabetics.

The foregoing discussion, diagrammed in Figure 4, leads to the conclusion that these are the most likely effects of HCA:

1. The passage of large amounts of carbohydrate metabolites through the liver, probably affecting glucoreceptors and reducing appetite as discussed below
2. The rapid and elevated production of glycogen (storage starch) in the liver and other tissues, again affecting glucoreceptors
3. The possible loss of significant amounts of energy as heat, and
4. The possible increase in normal thermogenesis through the actions of glucoreceptors in the liver.

In experimental studies, this cycle of events caused by HCA has led to reduced food consumption and to weight loss. Humans have reported elevated energy levels.

No significant tolerance and no rebound appeared in experimental studies. Over time, most diet products become less effective, a development called "tolerance." As is pointed out in the chapter "Why HCA Is Unique," HCA does not act on the central nervous system and its effectiveness does not appear to lessen except very slowly with time. In laboratory trials, minimal tolerance began to appear only after four or more weeks of chronic administration, depending upon the model of obesity used, i.e., whether genetic or otherwise induced in the test animals. In one trial, no tolerance had developed even after 80 days of continued ingestion of HCA. This makes HCA a very unusual product. Development of tolerance for HCA's effects would indicate that one of the alternate pathways across the mitochondrial membrane (see Figure 3) had become more active in response to the blockage of the citrate.[16]

INHIBITING LIPOGENESIS

Summary

By inhibiting the actions of ATP-citrate lyase, HCA reduces the availability of acetyl-CoA, the building block for fatty acid and cholesterol synthesis. This may also cause the body to remove some already circulating low-density lipoprotein (LDL) from the blood. The reduction in cholesterol synthesis is greater than the reduction in fatty acid synthesis. Animal trials have resulted in reductions in triglycerides, cholesterol, food consumption and weight gain. Two preliminary human studies produced similar results when chromium was added to HCA in the diet.

Figure 4. Partial Regulation of Glycolysis (Metabolism of Carbohydrates) and the Krebs Cycle by HCA

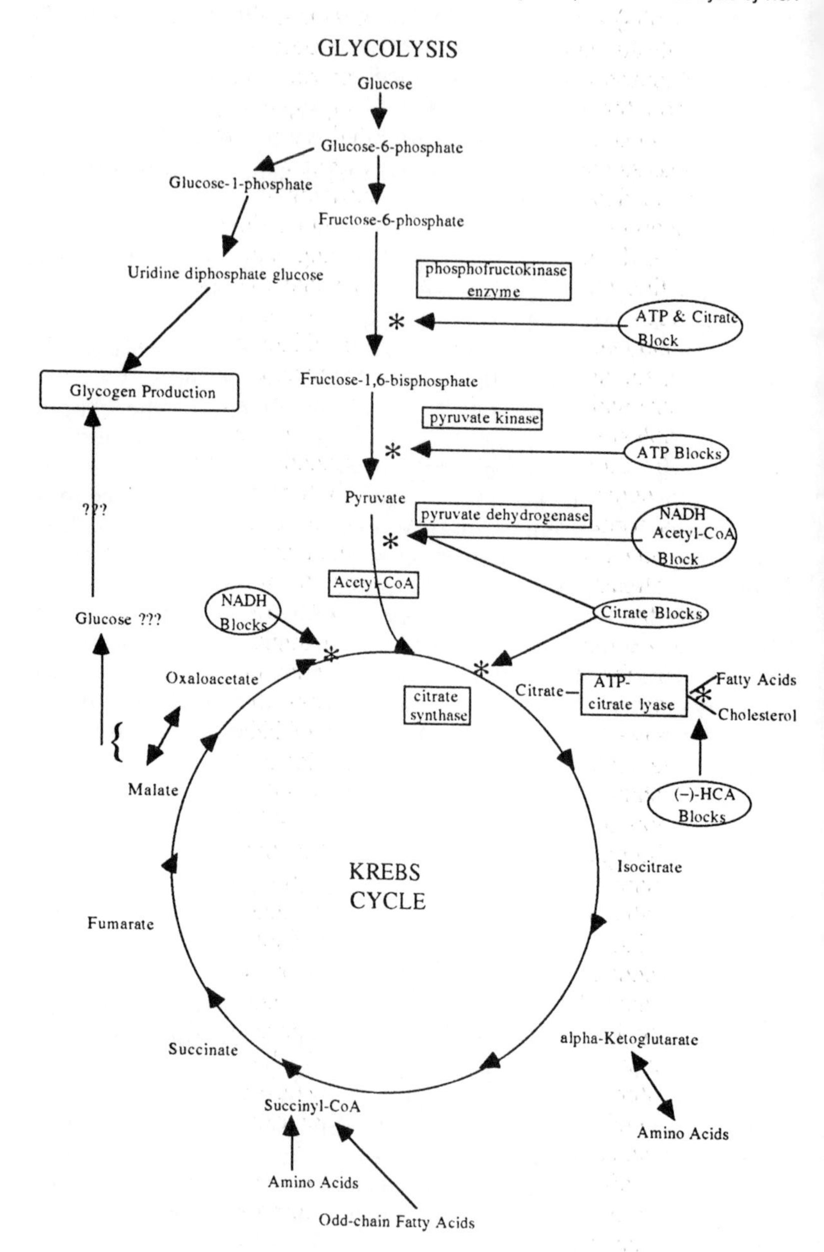

A decline in the activity of citrate as a carrier of acetyl groups (2-carbon units) across the mitochondrial membrane has a number of ramifications, several of which have been explored in animal studies. Perhaps the most significant of the effects of HCA is its impact upon the production of fats. Lipogenesis, the creation of fatty acids and cholesterol, is initiated very early in the Krebs Cycle as excess calories are directed out of the metabolic pathway via citrate as described above. By reducing the pool of available 2-carbon acetyl-CoA, HCA indirectly inhibits the synthesis of both cholesterol and triglycerides. *In vitro* testing with human liver hepatoma cell line Hep G2 cells has shown that the presence of HCA under various conditions consistently reduces cholesterol synthesis. HCA also leads to the up-regulation of low-density lipoprotein (LDL) receptor activity, with the concomitant increase in catabolism, i.e., removal, of LDL from the system, as a compensation for lowered cholesterol synthesis. Reduction of the primary production of cholesterol is roughly twice as effective as the reduction of triglyceride synthesis in Hep G2 cells, whereas in rat studies the impact was somewhat more equal. *The exact impact in vivo upon human cholesterol and triglyceride production is not known at present.* (As noted already, other pathways for the movement of acetyl-CoA across the mitochondrial membrane than through citrate may exist in the human liver, for instance, through acetoacetate.)[17]

It is certain that HCA in the cytosol activates a lipogenic enzyme known as acetyl-CoA carboxylase (as does the citrate which remains uncleaved because of the presence of HCA), and this action explains the unequal inhibitions of cholesterol and triglyceride syntheses established experimentally. Cholesterol synthesis is dependent upon a renewed supply of acetyl-CoA. With regard to the diminished pool of acetyl-CoA found in the presence of HCA, further biosynthesis gives preference to the production of non-cholesterol fatty acid biosynthesis, for instance, to palmitic acid.[18]

These conclusions regarding the effects of HCA on the synthesis of fats represent a great deal of detective work done over a period of several years. It could have been the case that even though HCA were to block the effects of ATP-citrate lyase and the link to the production of fats, this action would be circumvented in a subsequent step in the Krebs Cycle or through yet another mechanism. Lowenstein at Brandeis in a chapter published in *Essays in Cell Metabolism* (1970) was one of the first to point out the potential of HCA as an anti-lipogenic agent, and one year later he published a study which demonstrated that in live animals HCA reduces the synthesis of fatty acids as expected.[19] In 1972 the other side of lipid synthesis, the production of cholesterol, was examined in two papers which showed that this pathway is inhibited as well.[20]

It was at this point in time that scientists at Hoffmann-La Roche began to seriously examine the potential of HCA as an inhibitor of lipogenesis. A large team including Ann Sullivan (whose name became almost synonymous with HCA research) was brought together for this purpose. The researchers' first step was to again examine *in vitro* the relative effectiveness of the four stereoisomers of hydroxycitrate. (The lactone of HCA was obtained from the fruit of *Garcinia cambogia.*) Preliminary experiments satisfied them that of the four compounds, only (–)-hydroxycitrate was active. HCA was further examined first for its effects upon injection, and then acute oral administration. *The results were that "fatty acid and cholesterol synthesis were significantly inhibited by the oral administration of (–)-hydroxycitrate. . . ." but that the compound had to be given prior to feeding, preferably 30-60 minutes before, in order to be effective. The larger the amount of HCA given prior to feeding, the greater was the degree of reduction of lipogenesis. Finally, it was determined that (–)-hydroxycitrate and not the lactone is the active agent.*[21]

With this opening success, the team began other experiments. HCA had been shown to effectively inhibit lipogenesis when given in large dosages by mouth for a very short period of time, but it had yet to be established that this effect would continue with the chronic consumption of the extract. The Sullivan team wanted both to clarify the results of chronic use and to examine in greater detail the specific characteristics of lipogenesis inhibited by acute intake of HCA. The synthetic (G-70) diet fed to the experimental rats was designed to induce the production of fats. It consisted of 70 percent glucose, 23 percent vitamin-free casein (milk protein), 5 percent salt mixture, 1 percent corn oil, 1 percent vitamin mixture, and 40 g/kg of cellulose for fiber.[22]

The results of these trials were impressive. The acute oral dose of HCA (2.63 mmoles/kg equivalent to roughly 594 mg/kg body weight) given prior to the standardized synthetic meal caused a significant decrease in liver lipogenesis (*roughly 70 percent*) for up to eight hours after the meal. The production of lipids declined not only in the liver, but in the other tissues in which fats are formed from carbohydrates, i.e., in the small intestine and in adipose tissues. Lipogenesis returned to the levels found in the control animals after 12 hours, which indicated that the material had cleared the system by this time.

Various amounts of HCA were also given over a 30-day period (2.63, 1.32 and 0.66 mmoles/kg/day) to rats to judge the effects. The type of intervention in hepatic (liver) lipogenesis did not vary between the acute and the chronic feedings of HCA, and lipogenesis continued to be depressed during the 30-day period. A further result was that the animals fed HCA for the duration showed a considerable reduction in appetite and weight gain along with the reduction in lipogenesis. The use of pair-feedings in which control animals were restricted to the amount of food voluntarily eaten by the test animals served to prove that the reduction in lipogenesis could not be attributed to the reduction in food intake, but rather reflected the impact of the reduction in lipid formation. (Under other circumstances, as discussed below, Sullivan et al., however, found it difficult to conclude that the inhibition of lipogenesis *per se* rather than the reduction in appetite was the cause of reduced weight gain.) Of further interest is the finding that cells drawn from rats chronically fed HCA and then tested have elevated rates of lipids formation *if no new HCA is present.* However, when HCA was added to the cell culture, it again depressed fat synthesis in these cells—just as it did in the living animal. This indicated that the chronic inhibition of ATP-citrate lyase probably elevated the amount of that enzyme available in cells, but that HCA still suppressed the enzyme even after 30 days.

In 1977, researchers from Hoffmann-La Roche published several papers which addressed directly the impact of HCA on the production of various lipids, e.g., triglycerides, fatty acids, and cholesterol. In one of these studies, Ann C. Sullivan, Joseph Triscari and Herbert E. Spiegel investigated whether HCA could influence hypertriglyceridemia (high blood fat) which had resulted from both genetic and experimentally induced causes.[23] In Zucker obese rats, high serum triglyceride levels and high rates of lipids synthesis in comparison with the rates of their lean litter mates are genetically determined. In normal rats similar elevations of triglycerides and hepatic lipogenesis can be induced by a diet high in fructose. In a third experimental model, the substance Triton given intravenously also produces a rise in serum triglycerides, although increased lipid synthesis does not seem to be the cause in this case. The relevance of the rat hypertriglyceridemic models for humans is that in both species elevated triglycerides is a lipid disorder which can result from the excessive consumption of simple carbohydrates (especially fructose), poor clearance or utilization of triglycerides in peripheral tissues, or from an impaired response to carbohydrate/fat combinations. In all three models, HCA was successful in reducing serum triglyceride levels. Both in the Zucker obese model and in the fructose-induced model, fatty acid synthesis also was significantly reduced. Cholesterol levels were likewise reduced in these models.[24]

Results with HCA depend upon several factors, including the amount of fat and alcohol in the diet. Under experimental conditions, HCA reduces cholesterol synthesis at a rate greater than it reduces fatty acid synthesis. (See above.) These results are apparently somewhat species-specific in that mechanisms of circumventing ATP-citrate lyase or yet other regulatory mechanisms vary. In the rat, HCA powerfully inhibits cholesterol and other lipid syntheses,[25] yet this may not be true in chickens.[26] And even in animals in which the inhibition of lipid synthesis is effective, diet can play a negative role. Consumption of alcohol, for instance, may negate the effects of HCA in some mammals and actually increase fatty acid synthesis.[27] Even in the rat a diet high in fats may reduce the impact of HCA on fatty acid synthesis by reducing the role of citrate in general.[28] In one study a practical consequence of differing ratios of dietary fat and carbohydrates upon responses to (–)-hydroxycitrate was the total elimination of the expected anorexia.[29] HCA usually has a pronounced appetite-suppressing effect upon the rat, yet increased fat in the diet appeared to blunt this benefit.

Tests with human hepatoma cell line Hep G2 showed an inhibition of both fatty acid and cholesterol synthesis in response to HCA. The receptors for binding low-density lipoprotein also were up-regulated by HCA. The conclusion of the team of researchers was that "results suggest that the increases in HMG-CoA reductase [enzyme levels] and the LDL receptor are initiated by the decreased flux of carbon units in the cholesterol-synthetic pathway, owing to inhibition of ATP-citrate lyase."[30] In other words, the remaining cholesterol and fatty acid synthesis became dependent on substrates which already existed in the cells and the body compensated for the loss of its usual source of substrates by withdrawing and recycling already existing cholesterol. In effect, the total amount of cholesterol available was reduced.

These results were achieved with a cell line which is comparable in its metabolism to normal human liver cells. Clinical studies in humans are only now taking place, but preliminary clinical trials are suggestive, if not conclusive. In a published paper, A. Conte found that HCA given three times per day prior to meals for two months had a significant effect upon weight loss, which suggests that humans are indeed responsive to HCA.[31] In a second study (as yet unpublished), blood tests indicated that serum lipids levels are reduced in response to a combination of HCA and niacin-bound chromium. Since neither of these studies compares the results of HCA with and without the addition of chromium and other factors, a definitive answer to the impact of HCA on the production of fats in humans must await further trials.

SUPPRESSING THE APPETITE

Summary

Tests to establish the appetite-suppressing effects of HCA found that a single large oral dose or two divided oral doses totaling one-seventh the size of the single dose resulted in a 10 percent or greater reduction in food consumption in experimental animals fed a high-sugar diet. This result continued over many weeks with the chronic ingestion of HCA. The appetite control mechanism of HCA does not involve any conditioned aversion to food, i.e., HCA does not alter taste, cause gastric distress or illness, etc. Rather, this control stems from the increased production of glycogen and the concomitant stimulation of glucoreceptors in the liver, which results in early satiety through signals sent to the brain via the vagus nerve. Two preliminary human trials suggest that HCA may work better when combined with chromium and/or other insulin potentiators and/or mimics. Diets high in fat and alcohol will reduce the lipogenesis-inhibiting and appetite-suppressing effects of HCA.

(–)-Hydroxycitrate's inhibitive effect upon the biosynthesis of fats in animal experiments ranged from 40-70 percent of the production found in controls and this effect lasted less than 24 hours (and under some circumstances, less than 12 hours). One pair-feeding trial suggested that the reduction in lipogenesis itself accounted for differences in weight gain between animals consuming HCA and the controls. However, in subsequent published papers the Hoffmann-La Roche researchers generally concluded either that reduced food intake accounted for the reduced weight gain seen in their trials or that it was not useful to distinguish between the suppression of appetite and the suppression of lipogenesis as the causative factor.[32] Further work had made it clear that the same process which impeded the formation of fats from carbohydrate calories also was responsible for reducing appetite, although it was some time before scientists uncovered the actual physiologic mechanism which linked the two.

The Hoffmann-La Roche scientists investigated several issues related to appetite and weight gain by comparing the effects both of differing amounts of HCA and of different administration schedules used over a 30-day period. Again using a synthetic diet as described above, researchers fed groups of rats a single oral dose of HCA (trisodium salt form produced from the extract of *Garcinia cambogia*) once per day at the rates of 0.17, 0.66, 1.32 and

2.63 mmoles/kg. Another group of animals was given HCA twice per day at the rate of 0.33 mmoles/kg. These dosages were given one hour before meals. The result was that significant reductions in weight gain, food intake and total body lipids, but not in serum or liver lipids, were found in the rats fed 2.63 mmoles/kg once a day and in the rats fed 0.33 mmoles/kg twice per day. Indeed, by one measure the better results over the 30-day period were found with the twice per day administration of the lesser dosage than with the largest once-daily administration, although this was not true of the first 11 days. Over the entire period, results were roughly 700 percent greater for the amount of HCA administered when the extract was given twice per day rather than only once. In other experiments, it was shown that a sodium salt of citrate (i.e., of citric acid) had no effect upon weight gain or upon gains in body fat. Therefore, it was conclusive that the control of weight and body fat was specific to HCA and its impact upon the metabolism.[33]

The source of HCA's results, i.e., whether the lack of weight gain was due to an impedance in fat formation and storage or to a simple reduction in food intake, was examined by pair-feeding. For each animal given HCA, another animal was given a salt solution. Then the control animals (those receiving the saline solution) were restricted to exactly the same amount of food which voluntarily was consumed by the HCA-treated animals. Under these conditions, identical restrictions in weight gain and total body lipids were observed. The production of lipids in the liver itself was reduced in the HCA-treated partners in pair-feedings, but not in the control animals responding to the simple restriction in calories. *This meant that HCA reduced the weight gain by reducing food intake.* The reduction in appetite was a result of the inhibition of lipogenesis, to be sure, but the effect upon weight gain was indirect rather than direct. That this mechanism worked to prevent fat storage without interfering with normal growth at the dosages given was indicated by a later study which showed that in healthy normal growing rats the lean tissues of the HCA-treated animals did not differ in quantity from those found in controls.

Although it had been conclusively proven and accepted since 1969 that HCA inhibited the enzyme ATP-citrate lyase with the consequences outlined above, there remained the possibility that the inhibition of the citrate cleavage enzyme was not the mechanism responsible for the weight and lipid-reducing effects of HCA. For instance, the extract might have worked by altering the taste of food. (As an example of this phenomenon, a particular extract of the Indian herb *Gymnema sylvestre* can alter the taste perception of foods usually considered to be sweet.) If HCA worked through this type of mechanism, it might be useful as part of a "behavioral approach" to obesity[34] and yet not have much application to weight and/or body and blood fat problems which are not the result of behaviors. If HCA were shown to work by a more direct mechanism, then this extract's range of health uses likely would be greater.

Hoffmann-La Roche was aware of the possibility that HCA works through some sort of "conditioned aversion" to food. In a paper published in 1977, Ann Sullivan joined three psychologists from Bowling Green State University to test whether this was in fact the case.[35] This team was interested in discovering whether HCA had effects such as causing illness or gastrointestinal distress in response to food. These and other mechanisms could explain the experimentally observed reduction in appetite. A number of compounds, such as ethylenediamine and lithium chloride, work through such means.

The results with lithium chloride were, as expected, that this compound caused a strong rejection of a saccharine-flavored solution. The ethylenediamine salt of HCA likewise produced a strong aversion, albeit less so than the lithium chloride. The sodium salt of HCA produced aversions only under the most sensitive of conditions. Further testing showed that the aversive effects of the ethylenediamine salt of HCA were due entirely to the ethylenediamine itself and not to the HCA. Finally, the degree of appetite suppression found with the HCA compounds could not be explained as being a consequence of any aversive effects from HCA. In other words, HCA had been shown to reduce appetite through a mechanism which did not involve illness, distress or some other aversive response to food.

Most appetite suppressants work only for a few days before tolerance develops, yet the anorectic effects of HCA in treated animals lasted for weeks. Many appetite suppressants have the further disadvantage of leading to considerable rebound weight gain once treatment stops. Again, HCA appeared to avoid the common pitfall. *Even after 7 weeks of effective suppression of appetite in one trial, there was no rebound;* the weight of the treated animals remained less than that of the controls after the trial ended.[36] *Moreover, the degree of appetite suppression was considerable.* Treated animals ate at least 10 percent less food than did controls.[37]

The puzzle for scientists was that HCA did not work through mechanisms of which they were aware from their experience with other anorectic substances. One of the primary centers of satiety control, and the one with which they were most familiar, is the hypothalamus found deeply imbedded within the brain. Rats which have experimentally induced lesions in the hypothalamus become obese because of inadequate regulation of appetite. Nevertheless, these animals responded to treatment with HCA just as did other animal models of obesity. This fact led Sullivan and Triscari at Hoffmann-La Roche to suspect that another substance partially blocked by HCA through reductions in the pool of acetyl-CoA might be involved in appetite control. Since it was known that production of the neurotransmitter acetylcholine in the brain depended upon citrate as a precursor for acetyl-CoA, this pair of scientists speculated that HCA could be transported into the brain and the hypothalamus and thus influence satiety and hunger.[38] However, studies undertaken to establish this point found instead that *HCA does not readily cross the blood-brain barrier*, and therefore that it does not suppress appetite by acting directly upon the brain.[39]

Some new mechanism thus had to be found to explain the appetite suppression produced by HCA. The influence of HCA upon the production of fats in the liver suggested to researchers that this organ might actually be the key to HCA's capacity to reduce food intake. Experiments set up to examine this hypothesis discovered something rather remarkable: In animal trials, it was clear that treatment with HCA caused a significant increase in the production of glycogen in the liver (roughly 20 percent greater than in controls) for 6-10 hours after feedings, with no important elevation over that found in controls after 12 hours. (Glycogen is a special storage carbohydrate found in the liver and the muscles.) This meant that with the administration of HCA before feedings, some of the carbohydrate calories which under normal circumstances would be converted to fatty acids and cholesterol were instead converted to glycogen production and storage. The carbon units which citrate allows to leave the mitochondria had been prevented from doing so. Researchers had long speculated that the production of glycogen in both the liver and the small intestine played an important role in controlling appetite, and experiments with HCA strongly supported this hypothesis.[40]

These findings regarding HCA's mechanism for reducing the appetite have important implications for human usage. If the HCA-induced inhibition of lipid biosynthesis diverts the metabolism of carbohydrates toward glycogen production, the compound may not only reduce appetite, but also improve energy levels and blood sugar control in some cases.

The liver under normal circumstances, including the absence of diabetes, stores roughly 15 grams, perhaps more, of glucose as glycogen per kg (2.2 pounds) of body weight. It is usually estimated that 5-8 percent of the liver's total weight must be filled by glycogen stores before lipogenesis will commence.[41] Obese individuals are known to typically possess less glycogen storage and more triglyceride (fat) storage than do their nonobese counterparts.[42] The exact nature of the satiety control exerted by the liver is not known, but it is generally accepted that the rate of glucose oxidation and/or the size of glycogen stores activates hepatic glucoreceptor sites which, in turn, signal the ventromedial hypothalamus (the "satiety center") via the vagus nerve. Similar effects and controls also emanate from the small intestine.[43] As indicated by the case of experiments using lesioned-hypothalamus rats, the anorectic effect of HCA does not appear to be limited to influences upon the hypothalamus. This does not rule out a primary role for vagally innervated hepatic glucoreceptors; it merely means that the vagus nerve affects satiety in more than one way.

Considerable evidence exists to the effect that glycogen storage mechanisms in peripheral muscle tissues are defective in both obese and non-insulin dependent diabetics (NIDDs). It has been shown that glycogen storage mechanisms are similarly defective in the liver tissues of NIDDs as well.[44] Liver tests have not yet been performed to examine this issue with obese, but non-diabetic individuals. Nevertheless, indirect evidence can be marshaled to the effect that nondiabetic obese individuals commonly exhibit difficulties in liver glycogen production, as is indicated by the low relative levels of glycogen storage mentioned already. Certainly other parameters of liver function often are deficient in obese individuals.[45]

It may be the case that HCA will prove more effective in suppressing appetite and in improving energy levels when combined with nutrients which themselves influence blood glucose regulation and glycogen production and storage. Chromium, manganese and vanadium are three of many such substances which are known and readily available. The two human trials pursued by A. Conte mentioned previously did not test the effects of HCA used alone, but rather in combination with special nutrients. Of particular relevance in light of the known effect of HCA upon glycogen production is the use in the Conte trials of niacin-bound chromium as an adjunctive supplement to HCA. (This combination of nutrients has special application to blood sugar and blood lipid problems.) Conte's trials also limited the consumption of fats in the diet and encouraged the drinking of large amounts of water. Subjects reported both higher energy levels and appetite suppression. Over an eight-week period, subjects lost almost three times as much weight as controls (11.1 pounds versus 4.2 pounds). Other human trials using HCA matched with a relatively low-fat (less than 25 percent of calories) and low-alcohol diet (no more than two drinks per day) are in progress. It is likely that this protocol combined with insulin potentiators and/or insulin mimics will become standard in the employment of HCA.[46]

STIMULATING THERMOGENESIS?

Summary

A thermogenic (heat-generating) effect has been postulated to account for some of the weight loss found experimentally using HCA. There are both theoretical and experimental reasons for suspecting that this may take place and for suggesting that L-carnitine be used in conjunction with HCA. However, no actual trials have been conducted to test the hypothesis. Other methods which are known to improve thermogenesis in the overweight, such as supplementation with sufficient quantities of GLA (gamma-linolenic acid), potassium and magnesium, might be used in conjunction with HCA without causing unwanted central nervous system stimulation.

Some authors have speculated that HCA stimulates fat burning.[47] The basic argument rests upon both theoretical claims and recalcula-

Figure 5. Regulation of Food Intake (after Anderson)

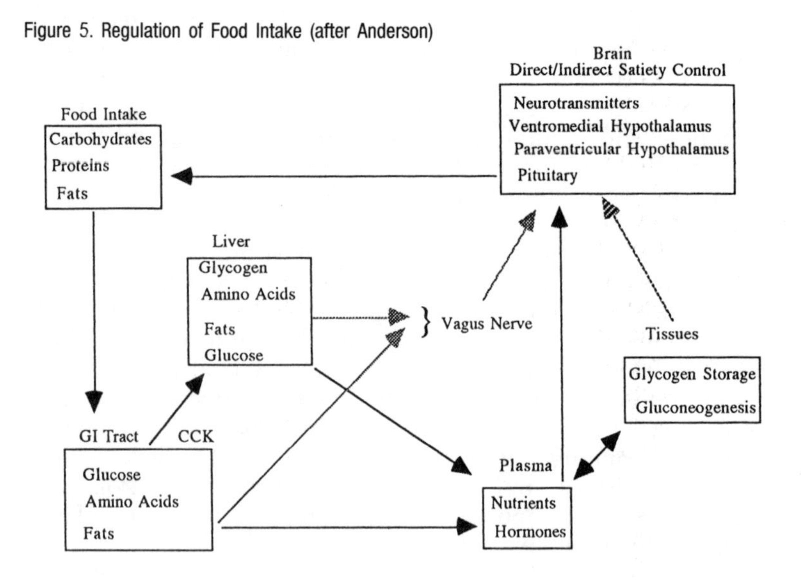

tions of data from the Hoffmann-La Roche studies. The former stress that the liver-induced glucoreceptor signals which travel via the vagus nerve to the brain may regulate the release of neurotransmitters which stimulate thermogenesis (the burning and release of excess calories as heat). The increased movement of carbohydrate products through the liver, the same movement which ultimately leads to increased glycogen production, might have this vagally mediated thermic effect. A second portion of this theoretical argument relies upon the claim that HCA stimulates gluconeogenesis, the conversion of certain non-carbohydrates (which would include pyruvate) to glucose as fuel for the brain and other activities or for storage in a calorie-wasteful cycle. This process expends energy as part of the chemical transformations involved. The general argument seems to be that if carbohydrate calories are prevented from being stored as fats, the metabolism of the acetyl groups which continue through the Krebs Cycle now as part of lipid oxidation will activate the enzymes which cause gluconeogenesis (the production of glucose from non-carbohydrate sources). Specifically, HCA funnels calories into the production of oxaloacetate, which is itself the first step in gluconeogenesis. Finally, as this rather elaborate argument runs, the addition of the amino acid L-carnitine to the HCA regimen will augment the thermogenic effect of the extract.

There is some experimental evidence for these conjectures. According to Mark McCarty, who has submitted an article on the topic to *Medical Hypotheses*, a rereading of evidence from the La Roche studies suggests that the reductions in weight gain found in these trials was significantly greater than the reductions in food consumption. If this contention is true, then the two most likely explanations are that treatment with HCA leads to either an increase in physical activity or an increase in thermogenesis. The production of increased glycogen, as described above, burns calories and generates some heat as a result of the chemical actions involved. An additional thermogenic effect of the classic sort, that is, thermogenesis from brown adipose tissue, would account for yet more of the experimental statistical discrepancies. This, of course, assumes that extra activity does not account for the statistical differences which McCarty has noted. Human subjects using HCA have reported greater energy along with the expected appetite suppression, and thus it is not obvious that thermogenesis is involved. Nevertheless, both processes might be involved in the energy expenditure which leads to weight loss with HCA.

A major weakness in the above hypothesis lies in the fact that most individuals with long-standing weight problems have difficulty in initiating thermogenesis because of insulin resistance and impaired response to the hormones which normally would cause a thermic effect with the consumption and metabolism of food. Excess tissue in the form of fat stores readily encourages insulin resistance, and insulin resistance alone is capable of reducing the thermic response to food.[48] HCA might benefit these individuals by reducing their production of fats in response to carbohydrate calories, but this is not a direct thermic effect. More generally in humans, weight loss which is not accompanied by a dramatic loss of lean tissue tends to be thermogenic for the quite simple reason that decreased insulation around the waist in the form of fat under the skin allows the dissipation of the heat produced by thermogenesis. Thermogenesis is dependent upon the body's regulation of internal or core temperature, and excess fat interferes with this regulation.

The notion that HCA might enhance the thermogenic response to food is an intriguing one. The particular argument presented by McCarty may not hold for the simple reason that HCA most likely regulates carbohydrate metabolism long before the oxaloacetate/gluconeogenesis nexus is reached. This is to say that HCA funnels carbohydrate calories toward glycogen production before these calories actually run through the Krebs Cycle. Nevertheless, any increased flux of carbohydrate metabolites through the liver may activate thermogenesis. Not all of the mechanisms involved in thermogenesis are known.[49] It remains the case that experimental data either confirming or disconfirming a thermogenic effect for HCA do not yet exist.

There are other ways to reactivate the body's basic ability to respond to sympathetic neural stimulation—its ability to respond to food intake with a slight rise in body temperature—and therefore to take advantage of HCA's ability to reduce the storage of calories as fat. One way of doing this is to supplement with the special fatty acid GLA (gamma-linolenic acid) derived from the evening primrose oil, borage oil or black currant seed oil.[50] Another route is to add a sufficient amount of the minerals potassium and magnesium to the diet. Since HCA can be provided as a salt of either of these alkali minerals, supplementation with HCA and the minerals might even be accomplished with the same supplement. As is the case with GLA, only more quickly, potassium and magnesium (and, much more questionably, phosphorous) reactivate the enzyme Na/K ATPase, which is the enzyme key to the body's thermic brown fat response to increased glucose in the blood plasma and, perhaps, its response to adrenal hormones.[51]

IS HCA SAFE?

TOXICOLOGY, TOLERANCE AND DOSAGE

Toxicity tests have been conducted to verify the absence of possible side effects or acute/chronic toxicity of the HCA isolate.[52] The results showed that the acute LD_{50} (lethal dose for 50 percent of the animals tested) was greater than 2000 mg/kg for intraperitoneal administration and greater than 4000 mg/kg for oral administration. The researchers at Hoffmann-La Roche achieved very similar results using simple citrate and considered the two compounds almost identical in safety. The Merck Index lists the LD_{50} of citrate used intraperitoneally as 975 mg/kg, which would indicate that HCA is actually safer than citrate. However, this comparison may simply reflect differing methodologies used for the tests. Other tests covering the safety of HCA for various tissues, i.e., the liver, blood, and so forth, are now being performed at various centers.

With regard to safety, the significant points are these: First, HCA and citrate are very close in terms of their degree of safety, and the latter is now used freely in the preparation of many foods and drinks. And, of course, citrate is the primary acid in oranges, lemons and other citrus fruits. Second, *Garcinia cambogia,* as described in the section on botany and traditional uses, has a long history of employment as a flavoring, preservative and herbal tonic. A typical daily dose of HCA in humans for the purpose of losing weight is roughly the equivalent of the rind of half a fruit, which is an insignificant amount considering its common use. Reports of toxicity simply do not appear in the literature regarding traditional use of the extract, so it is highly unlikely that there is any danger from regular consumption. The most likely negative effect from excess intake of the isolate would be bowel intolerance, and this problem would be reversible through a simple reduction in dosage. However, this problem was not seen in animal studies at the levels of intake which were necessary to reduce appetite.

Despite its inherent safety, there are individuals who should not use HCA, just as they should not use any other diet product. HCA influences the body's own production of cholesterol, and therefore it may influence indirectly the production of sterols. The hormones made from sterols include estrogen, progesterone, testosterone and so forth. For the great majority of Americans, the diet is so rich in fats and in calories in general that a lack of building blocks for fat-dependent hormones within the body is simply not an issue. Nevertheless, some instances require caution.

Pregnancy is a time of extreme sensitivity to steroid hormones, and therefore products which contain HCA should not be used during pregnancy. HCA should be avoided during lactation. Similarly, HCA should not be given in large amounts or for extended periods of time to young children.

Although long human experience with fruit sources of HCA does not indicate any danger to these groups, it must be remembered that fruit sources consist almost totally of the less active lactone of HCA.

Animal trials, as described above, have indicated very little development of tolerance (i.e., of HCA becoming less effective with time) even at relatively high intakes of the isolate. In some cases the beginning of tolerance was seen after 30 days, but in others there was no decrease in anorectic effects even after 80 days. *Therefore, the development of tolerance may not prove to be of great importance with HCA.*

Establishing a proper dosage level for HCA is more difficult. *The two Conte studies (one published, one still being analyzed) found good results when 250 mg of HCA as a calcium salt was given three times per day before meals, i.e., a total of 750 mg of HCA per day.* These studies included other important factors such as niacin-bound chromium in their test supplement, and therefore it is difficult to guess what dosage would be effective without at least adding chromium or some other insulin potentiator to the formula. Extrapolations from animal data suggest that a more significant effect from HCA would require an average-sized human to consume 3-6 grams per day in 1-2 gram dosages taken 30-60 minutes before meals.

A CAVEAT REGARDING THE USE OF HCA FOR GENETIC OBESITY

Most Americans with weight control problems are not overweight because of purely genetic, that is, inherited metabolic patterns, although these can be quite important. As a rule, poor nutrition, lack of exercise, improper food choices and eating habits are more significant for weight gain than is genetics in the narrow sense.

Nevertheless, it is worth noting the experimental evidence for what HCA can and what it cannot accomplish with a certain type of genetically controlled weight problem.

When HCA was studied for its effects upon on the development of obesity in the genetically obese Zucker rat, the results were somewhat mixed. In this study, lean (Fa/-) and genetically obese (fa/fa) Zucker female rats were fed HCA as a dietary admixture for 39 days (52.6 mmoles/kg diet). The diet used was the synthetic G-70 diet based upon glucose described previously. In the lean rats, HCA decreased body weight, food intake, percent of body fat, and fat cell size. In the obese rats, food intake and body weight were reduced, but the percent of body tissues devoted to fat remained unchanged. Obese rats maintained a fat cell size equivalent to their obese controls throughout the treatment period. There was a reduction in fat cell number in the obese rats treated with HCA during the period of the trial. However, there also was a marked reproliferation of fat cells in the post-treatment period. These results indicated that although HCA treatment substantially reduced body weight, the genetically obese rats still maintained their genetically determined ratio of fat-to-lean tissues.[53]

As already noted, the implications of this study for those with a family history of obesity are mixed. HCA did successfully reduce weight in this animal model, but it did not improve the encoded ratio of fat-to-lean tissue. Other means, including a weight-training program, may be useful in humans with similar problems, but dieting alone will not prove entirely satisfactory.

WHY HCA IS UNIQUE

One of the reasons that HCA was the focus of so much interest at Hoffmann-La Roche was that it offered a unique peripheral approach to controlling weight gain. Numerous pharmacological strategies have been applied in the past to the manipulation of appetite and the treatment of obesity, but the regulation of appetite is a complex process which has largely resisted intervention. Rather unfortunately, all currently available anorectic drugs act by central nervous system mechanisms and have several disadvantages, including limited effectiveness, side effects involving the nervous system, elevated or irregular heartbeat, elevated blood pressure, often a rapid development of tolerance, potential for abuse (including addictive qualities), and rebound hyperphagia—the "yo-yo" effect of the body rapidly regaining all the weight lost with a product or diet when that regimen is discontinued. HCA avoids these problems because it acts locally at the level of carbohydrate metabolism and through the liver to influence appetite via the vagus nerve.

There are three main categories of approaches now in use to manipulate the appetite. The first of these involves catecholamine pathways, which means central nervous system (CNS) pathways which depend upon neurotransmitters and the hormones which release these. Many or even most of the catecholamines used in weight management are part of the "fight or flight" mechanisms of the body. Just as this implies, their use leads to great stress on the body. The centrally acting (i.e., CNS) anorectics include amphetamine, methamphetamine, phenmetrazine, phentermine, diethylpropion, fenfluramine, phenylpropanolamine, and mazindol. Most of these are phenylethylamine derivatives and are structurally related to the catecholamine neurotransmitters dopamine and norepinephrine. Norepinephrine causes the release of epinephrine, which is more commonly known as adrenaline. (Mazindol is not a phenylethylamine.)

In the health food industry, the current fashion for thermogenic diet products using the Chinese herb *Ma huang* makes use of another central nervous system stimulant. As even its Latin name indicates, *Ephedra sinica* supplies a natural form of ephedrine, which is a mimic of epinephrine, i.e, adrenaline. Ma huang can certainly increase thermogenic weight loss, but its long-term use will exhaust the body and lead to free-radical damage unless great caution is exercised. In the hands of a competent physician ephedrine-based products are quite useful and safe, but consumers should be aware of the necessity to cycle such products and to use additional antioxidants and other safeguards. All of these CNS agents, except fenfluramine, interact with catecholamine systems by either preventing the reuptake or enhancing the release of dopamine and norepinephrine to produce appetite suppressant effects. Those which either cause the release of adrenaline or mimic the effects of adrenaline themselves also act directly through a biochemical pathway to prevent the storage of fats.

A second approach to appetite control involves what are known as serotoninergic pathways. Fenfluramine acts similarly to the foregoing upon the central nervous system, only in this case the substance serves to release the neurotransmitter serotonin. The essential amino acid tryptophan is a precursor of serotonin in that it is an actual building block for the neurotransmitter. This amino acid, as would be expected, itself influences appetite. It is interesting that now that the FDA has excluded tryptophan from the market, a large number of artificial substitutes for it are being researched at various pharmaceutical houses as appetite control agents.

High concentrations of binding sites for all of these neurotransmitters are found in the hypothalamus and brain stem, areas known to be involved in the regulation of appetite and food consumption. Patient response to the effects of centrally active (CNS) anorectic agents is generally not robust. Studies have shown that all of the anorectic drugs will enhance weight loss by only about 0.5 lb/week compared to placebos, and many have negligible effects upon the desire for sweets.[54] Some of the thermogenic combinations, particular those which combine Ma huang with caffeine and aspirin or aspirin-like herbal extracts have yielded better results, but they still have serious side effects of which the public is generally unaware.

In addition to the CNS-dependent anorectics, there is another class of anorectic agents with a peripheral mechanism of action. The gastric hormone CCK (cholecystokinin), which is released high in the small intestine, has a profound inhibitory effect on food intake and is thought to send a satiety signal to the brain via the gastric branch of the vagus nerve. Notoriously, tolerance to the anorectic effect of CCK develops within hours! Other peripherally active anorectic agents serve as metabolic modifiers to reduce the rate of gastric emptying. One of the Hoffmann-La Roche spin-offs of research on HCA is (–)-*threo*-chlorocitric acid. This compound drastically slows the speed at which food leaves the stomach and enters the small intestine. Needless to say, it tends to depress the appetite. However, it is a true synthetic drug, and one which has yet to be released onto the market. The same observations regarding mode of action and unproven safety can be made of another related compound, epoxyaconitate.[55]

The list could be lengthened somewhat by including a consideration of the opiate-receptor blocker naloxone, new thermogenic agents and still more agents which block the utilization of calories. However, most of these have proven to have drawbacks when given to patients. Most also have proven disappointing, as well, in actual weight control. In particular, rebound weight gain is typically a problem with pharmaceutical agents, and our knowledge of weight gain simply does not justify the heavy-handed intervention into the body's natural processes which all drugs involve.[56]

Finally, there are the natural substances, L-tyrosine, L-glutamine and so forth which can have positive effects upon appetite suppression without the side effects found with drugs. However, these again act by way of CNS mechanisms and they do not work for everyone.

The most significant fact about HCA as a diet product is that it suppresses the appetite without affecting the central nervous system. Only (–)-hydroxycitrate, of all the peripherally acting anorectic agents, is found as a natural constituent of foods which have been regularly and copiously consumed by humans for a period of half a millenium. The non-centrally active properties of HCA mean that HCA does not increase nervousness nor does it interfere with sleep. It does not cause depression. It does not increase the production of free radicals within the nervous system as do most stimulants and thermogenic agents. It does not exhaust the body's supply of substrates for adrenal hormone production, as is true of the synthetic substance phenylpropanolamine (PPA), the most common over-the-counter appetite suppressant. It does not increase the loss of magnesium from the system, as do stimulants and ephedrine-containing products. It does not increase the loss of calcium, as caffeine commonly does in women. It does not interfere with joint repair and with the repair of the stomach lining, as do products which contain aspirin or aspirin analogs.

Instead of acting upon the central nervous system, HCA works peripherally by increasing the production and storage of glycogen in the liver. This is a fundamentally healthful physiological process which is impaired in many individuals with weight control problems. HCA accomplishes its results without ever entering the brain or causing the release of adrenal or other hormones.

CHOOSING THE RIGHT PRODUCT

QUALITY CONTROL

Potential users of HCA products should keep in mind that the effects of the extract depend upon the amount ingested. This turns out to be a significant issue because some products on the market contain very little actual HCA. Indeed, there are items being sold which are merely the ground dried rind of the fruit of *Garcinia cambogia* or *Garcinia indica.* Others consist almost entirely of the lactone of HCA, the form of HCA which has the least activity in the body.

The dried fruit rinds of *G. cambogia* and its relative contain HCA almost entirely in the form of the lactone. Further, the highest natural yield of the rind, a concentration rarely seen, is 30 percent lactone by weight. This means that an unextracted source will never contain greater than 30 percent HCA as lactone, and more commonly the range will be from 4-6 percent with the species *G. indica* to about 15 percent with *G. cambogia.* Products which look very dark and gritty probably are no more than the ground rind and should be avoided.

HCA can be made available as an acid dissolved in liquid, as an HCA lactone and as a salt of HCA. Theoretically, the liquid HCA would be the preferred form, but in fact it turns out to be next to impossible to bring this item to the market without its having already turned into its lactone, and the lactone is not the desired form. (This point will be discussed shortly.) Then there is the further difficulty of accurately measuring the concentration of HCA being provided in the liquid and salt forms. Many products which claim to be 50 percent HCA are really only 50 percent acids, which means a mixture of HCA along with whatever other acids are present. There are many organic acids other than HCA which can be found in the rind of *G. cambogia.*

Various analytic methods can be used to determine the HCA levels of products. In principle, the HCA content of a material can be analyzed by simply calculating the degree of acidity of the pertinent fraction of the product. This is called a "titration." Different acids have slightly different degrees of acidity, i.e., the acetic acid in vinegar is more acid than the malic acid found in apples, but less acid than the hydrochloric acid found in our stomachs. Unfortunately, what is simple in theory is often impossible in practice. A mixture of acids with closely related pH values, meaning very close degrees of acidity, when plotted on a graph will create an overlapping and difficult to interpret picture. Any manufacturer using such an approach will have a poor notion of the true quality of the product and will overstate the HCA content by a wide margin because this method is more useful for determining the total acid content than for determining any particular element within a group of similar acids. If any other acids are used in the extraction process, the testing procedure becomes even more difficult.

Two other methods which are far more reliable than titration are the HPLC (high-performance liquid chromatography, sometimes also called high-pressure liquid chromatography) method and the GCMS (gas chromatography mass spectroscopy) method. Each of these methods can be calibrated very finely to reveal both the presence of specific acids and the amount of each acid present. In the opinion of many experts in the field of chemistry, HPLC is the method preferred for the testing of (–)-hydroxycitric acid products. For instance, this is the judgment of Dr. Robert Rosen, Director of the Mass Spectrometry Laboratory at the Center for Advanced Food Technology, Department of Food Science, Rutgers University, and likewise of Dr. Bruce Branchaud, Associate Professor of Chemistry at the University of Oregon.

Whenever either of these methods are used, their reliability depends primarily upon two factors: 1) the quality of the laboratory doing the testing, and 2) the quality of the standard of the material used as a reference. In fact, the determining issue commonly is the second of these. Special chemical supply houses exist whose chief business is to supply pure forms of different chemicals for those who are interested in determining the purity of their products. In the case of HCA, this means that the standard for analysis must come from a reputable source, such as Hoffmann-La Roche, because HCA is difficult to acquire in pure form other than as its lactone.

LIQUID OR SALT? THE ISSUE OF THE HCA LACTONE

From the analysis given earlier, it is clear that HCA in its form as an analogue to citric acid is the active inhibitor of fat production and the initiator of increased glycogen production and storage. The Hoffmann-La Roche researchers decided in 1972 that for maximal effect when given by mouth, a sodium salt was more effective than the lactone,[57] and after that point the lactone ceased to be used in their studies. The next year, an independent group of scientists at the University of Toronto and at York University came to much the same conclusion. Free HCA proved to be roughly an order of magnitude more effective as an inhibitor of ATP-citrate lyase than did HCA lactone.[58] Most significantly, the original author of the Hoffmann-La Roche patent on the use of HCA for weight control, John M. Lowenstein at Brandeis University, in an article which he co-authored in 1981, states simply that the lactone "shows little or no inhibition of lipogenesis."[59]

So a customer should buy a liquid product offering HCA in its acid form, right? Well, not exactly. The problem which is encountered with HCA in its free form is that it is not stable. (Refer back to Figure 1.) Hoffmann-La Roche in its literature remarks, "In solution, compound slowly lactonizes to RO 20-1569 (about 10 percent in 7 days at 20 degrees)." This means that the pure solution of free HCA turns into its lactone at the rate of about 10 percent per week at low room temperature when in liquid form. The rate of conversion may slow as the concentration decreases, but there is little reason to expect that it stops entirely even at low concentrations, and higher temperatures definitely increase the rate of conversion. Definitive studies are currently being undertaken on this issue. As we know, free HCA is apparently not found in nature. Inasmuch as no one denies that only free HCA actually inhibits lipogenesis, the remaining issue is one of the degree to which the lactone is returned to the free acid form upon reaching the alkali environment of the small intestine after being consumed.

The only way known at present fully to stabilize HCA in its non-lactonized form is to combine it with an alkali mineral (such as calcium, potassium or sodium) to produce a salt of HCA. This is essentially an extension of the procedure which was originally used to remove HCA in its lactone form from the rinds of *Garcinia cambogia.* The lactone was returned to its free form by being dissolved in an alkali solution made from either sodium or potassium, and then the alkali mineral was removed. Any alkali mineral, such as calcium, can be used for this purpose, which is to open up and effect hydrolysis upon the rings which are closed in the lactone form. If the HCA is left in combination with the calcium salt, this will prevent the acid from again closing back upon itself to reform the lactone.

The bottom line, then, is that the best way to get free HCA may be to use a salt form of the compound. A properly prepared high-quality salt of HCA, such as calcium HCA, likely will prove both more stable and more active than the liquid form. The discerning consumer should examine the label for a listing of ingredients and select accordingly.

Finally, since HCA salts are fairly soluble, it may be possible to deliver a stable HCA product in liquid form even if further testing confirms that HCA in its free acid form cannot be used. Tests are now being done to determine the degree of "dissociation" which takes place when salts of HCA are placed in liquids. Dissociation refers to the separation of the molecule of HCA from its stabilizing alkali mineral. If the dissociation is not great, then the salt forms can be used in liquid products without significant transformation into the lactone.

COMPLEMENTARY NUTRIENTS

The complementary nutrients and other products appropriate for use along with HCA will depend on what the consumer is attempting to accomplish. For instance, dieters might focus primarily upon appetite regulation, but also be interested in increasing thermogenesis. Other users may want to explore HCA's potential for controlling blood lipid levels. At the opposite end of the spectrum from dieters, athletes might find the compound useful under some circumstances to improve energy levels. The following suggestions are not meant to offer medical advice, but merely to provide information which will allow purchasers of HCA products to better judge how these might be used and supplemented.

As a diet aid, HCA works primarily by increasing the production and storage of glycogen, and this fact provides the key to increasing the compound's appetite-suppressing effects. The hormone insulin plays a significant role in all aspects of glucose metabolism. It works in part by increasing the ability of glucose to cross cell membranes and in part by activating the pathways of carbohydrate metabolism within the cells, including the pathway to glycogen production. Therefore, supplements which support the role of insulin in the body should support the actions of HCA.

As a rule, individual with weight control problems are somewhat insensitive to the effects of insulin. Often even seemingly healthy individuals turn out to be insulin-resistant, a problem which Dr. Gerald Reaven of Stanford University calls "Syndrome X." Individuals who are insulin-resistant commonly fail to respond properly to rises in blood glucose which take place early during meals. This results in a slow and depressed satiety response to food consumption. Put simply, there is a tendency to eat more than one otherwise would because the signals which should have been received by the brain early in the meal are slow to arrive.

These same individuals likely suffer the further complication of a hyperglycemic/hypoglycemic roller coaster. The amount of glucose in their blood climbs to too high a level before their insulin succeeds in initiating regulation, and then the overshoot of insulin causes blood sugar levels to drop too low. The over-regulation depresses their basal rate of metabolism and reduces the number of calories which they should naturally burn during the course of the day.

When HCA increases the flux of carbohydrate metabolites through the liver, it influences the vagus nerve, which is a direct route to the satiety center in the brain. Substances which either potentiate insulin, such as chromium, or themselves mimic the effects of insulin, such as certain vanadium compounds, increase the movement of carbohydrate metabolites through the liver and increase the rate of glycogen production and perhaps its quantity of storage. The two clinical trials conducted by A. Conte mentioned earlier both combined HCA with niacin-bound chromium and other essential nutrients to good effect. It is theoretically likely that Conte achieved his results with lower dosages of HCA than otherwise would have been needed by using small amounts of insulin-potentiators. Further and more rigorous studies need to be conducted to clarify this point. Aside from chromium and vanadium compounds, other nutrients and extracts which might be used for the purpose of augmenting the response to HCA include manganese, vitamin B6, and the herbs *Gymnema sylvestre*, bitter melon, cloves and turmeric. Less direct in their effects, but nevertheless valuable in this regard are magnesium, potassium, zinc, vitamin B12 and folic acid.[60] All of these items are involved in carbohydrate metabolism and can be used to good advantage to improve insulin response.

It should be remembered that a number of nutrients influence appetite. The amino acids L-tyrosine and L-phenylalanine moderately elevate mood and reduce appetite by increasing the quantity of certain neurotransmitters in the brain. Some nutrient-dense foods, such as spirulina, have similar effects. Since the mechanisms involved differ from those of HCA, the effects may be additive.

Aside from appetite suppression, there is the possibility of increasing thermogenesis. Thermogenesis is another aspect of carbohydrate metabolism which is insulin-sensitive. Therefore most of the nutrients which improve the glycogen production and storage aspects of metabolism influenced by HCA will likewise help in some minor way with returning the thermic response which should come with each meal. Much more dramatic results can be expected, however, if a source of gamma-linolenic acid (GLA) is added to the diet. GLA is found in evening primrose oil, borage seed oil and black currant seed oil. The combination of the minerals magnesium and potassium, with the possible addition of phosphorous, similarly has been shown to greatly increase the activity of the enzyme which activates brown adipose tissue to generate thermogenesis. Since the amino acid L-carnitine sometimes is a rate-limiting factor in thermogenesis— L-carnitine is a "conditionally essential nutrient" which the body does not always produce enough of on its own—supplementing with L-carnitine often is helpful for increasing the mobilization and the burning of fat for heat.

Blood lipid problems, like weight problems, often are linked to insulin regulation. Vitamins B3 (niacin) and B6 and the minerals listed already, especially chromium, vanadium, copper and zinc, all have been shown to positively influence the levels of low-density lipoprotein (LDL), high-density lipoprotein (HDL) and triglycerides found in the blood. Many of these nutrients are synergistic in their effects. For instance, quite small amounts of vitamin B3 (niacin) are effective in controlling cholesterol levels when taken in conjunction with chromium. Individuals interested in controlling excess blood lipids also should explore the well-established role of antioxidants in helping with blood fat levels. The vitamins C and E and the amino acids L-carnitine and L-lysine are now suggested by leading authorities as being strongly protective in this regard.[61]

Athletes may be interested in HCA for its glycogen-enhancing effects. The supplement vanadyl sulfate is already widely used because it improves recovery and increases the feeling of fullness in the muscles when used properly with a carbohydrate-rich diet. The appetite-suppressing aspects of HCA will need to be weighed against its glycogen-storage effect, of course, as will the possible inhibition of the production of sterol precursors. Body builders in their "cutting up" stage may find the product useful, as might athletes in weight-sensitive sports, such as wrestling. HCA probably will prove less useful in the strictly anabolic cycles of sports training. More research needs to be done in the area of athletic supplementation with HCA.

It should be kept in mind that optimal dosage levels of HCA have yet to be established. Extrapolations from experimental data suggest that dosages in the range of 3-6 grams daily taken in 1-2 gram amounts 30-60 minutes before meals will prove most effective. Only minor modifications in the daily diet are needed to improve HCA's benefits. However, high-fat diets (those obtaining over 30 percent of their calories from fats) and high levels of alcohol consumption (more than two glasses of wine or two bottles of beer a day) will interfere with the effects of HCA.

CONCLUSION

(–)-Hydroxycitric acid is one of the most promising natural products to appear in many years. It has been extensively researched at leading universities and by the pharmaceutical giant Hoffmann-La Roche. Long used in large amounts as a condiment for foods, HCA has no toxicity, either acute or chronic, at any reasonable level of consumption. In this regard it is virtually identical to citric acid, the acid found in oranges, lemons and other citrus fruits. HCA works as a "partitioning agent" with calories obtained from carbohydrates, and, to a lesser extent, those from proteins. It diverts these calories away from the production of fats and toward the production of glycogen.

The health benefits of HCA are many. HCA inhibits lipogenesis, which is the production of fats from excess calories derived from carbohydrates and proteins. As an aspect of its regulation of lipogenesis, HCA lowers the production of both triglycerides and cholesterol. HCA increases the production and storage of glycogen in the liver and other tissues. By doing so, it increases energy levels while giving better control over the appetite. Finally, HCA may increase thermogenesis, the burning of calories for heat.

HCA therefore is potentially of great benefit to dieters and to others who are concerned with controlling their weight, including athletes. It may help individuals with problems with elevated blood fat levels. And in general, because of its effects upon glycogen production and storage, HCA likely will improve energy levels in many individuals who otherwise do not see themselves as having weight or blood fat problems.

SUMMARY OF THE BENEFITS OF HCA

- Decreased synthesis of fats, including triglycerides and cholesterol
- Increased clearance of LDL cholesterol
- Increased production of glycogen
- Reduced appetite
- Little or no development of tolerance
- No rebound ("yo-yo") weight gain after discontinuance
- Possible increase in thermogenesis
- Safe for diabetics
- Safe for extended consumption
- Long-term consumption contraindicated only for pregnant/lactating women and young children
- Does not stimulate the central nervous system
- Does not cross the blood-brain barrier
- Can be mixed with other nutrients to further enhance benefits.

REFERENCES

1. T. A. Wadden and A. J. Stunkard, "Psychosocial consequences of obesity and dieting," *Obesity: Theory and Therapy*, 2nd edition (New York: Raven Press, Ltd., 1993); *Nutrition Overview* III, 1 (1988).
2. Mark F. McCarty, "Promotion of Hepatic Lipid Oxidation and Gluconeogenesis as a Strategy for Appetite Control," *Medical Hypotheses* (1994, in press).
3. *The Wealth of India* (Raw Materials), vol. IV (New Delhi: Council Sci. Ind. Res., 1956) 99; Y. S. Lewis and S. Neelakantan, "(–)-Hydroxycitric Acid—the Principal Acid in the Fruits of *Garcinia Cambogia* Desr.," *Phytochemistry* 4 (1965) 619.
4. Ibid.; also Lily M. Perry with Judith Metzger, *Medicinal Plants of East and Southeast Asia* (Cambridge, Mass.: The MIT Press, 1980) 174–176; Vasant Lad and David Frawley, *The Yoga of Herbs* (Santa Fe: Lotus Press, 1986) 216.
5. W. Sergio, "A Natural Food, Malabar Tamarind, May Be Effective in the Treatment of Obesity," *Medical Hypotheses* 27 (1988) 40.
6. Ibid.
7. See note 3 above; see also Y. S. Lewis and S. Neelakantan, *Current Sci. India* 33 (1964) 82.
8. Y. S. Lewis, "Isolation and Properties of Hydroxycitric Acid," in John M. Lowenstein, ed., *Citric Acid Cycle*, vol. XIII in the series Methods in Enzymology (New York: Academic Press, 1969) 613–619; Per M. Boll, Else Sørensen and Erik Balieu, "Naturally Occurring Lactones and Lactames. III. The Absolute Configuration of the Hydroxycitric Acid Lactones: Hibiscus Acid and Garcinia Acid," *Acta Chemica Scandinavica* 23 (1969) 286–293.
9. John A. Watson, Marie Fang and John M. Lowenstein, "Tricarballylate and Hydroxycitrate: Substrate and Inhibitor of ATP: Citrate Oxaloacetate Lyase," *Archives of Biochemistry and Biophysics* 135 (1969) 200–217.
10. John M. Lowenstein, "Experiments with (–)-Hydroxycitrate," in W. Bartley, H. L. Kornberg and J. R. Quayle, eds., *Essays in Cell Metabolism* (London: Wiley–Interscience, 1970) 153–166; John M. Lowenstein, "Effect of (–)-Hydroxycitrate on Fatty Acid Synthesis by Rat Liver *in Vivo*," *The Journal of Biological Chemistry* 246, 3 (February

10, 1971) 629–632; H. Brunengraber, J. R. Sabine, Mireille Boutry and J. M. Lowenstein, "3-β-Hydroxysterol Synthesis by the Liver," *Archives of Biochemistry and Biophysics* 150 (1972) 392–396.

11. United States Patent Number 3,764,692 filed in 1970, accepted in 1973, and now expired.
12. Y. S. Lewis, 1969; see also John M. Lowenstein and Henri Brunengraber, "Hydroxycitrate," in John M. Lowenstein, ed., *Lipids*, vol. 72 in Methods in Enzymology (New York: Academic Press, 1981) 486–497; another analysis of the configuration of the hydroxycitrate isomers can be found in Ann C. Sullivan, *et al.*, "Reactivity and Inhibitor Potential of Hydroxycitrate Isomers with Citrate Synthase, Citrate Lyase and ATP Citrate Lyase," *The Journal of Biological Chemistry* 252, 21 (1977) 7583–7590.
13. Watson, *et al.*, 1969; A. C. Sullivan, J. G. Hamilton, *et al.*, "Inhibition of Lipogenesis in Rat Liver by (–)-Hydroxycitrate," *Archives of Biochemistry and Biophysics* 150 (1972) 183–190; A. C. Sullivan and J. Triscari, "Metabolic Regulation as a Control for Lipid Disorders. I. Influence of (–)-Hydroxycitrate on Experimentally Induced Obesity in the Rodent," *The American Journal of Clinical Nutrition* 30 (1977) 767–776; A. C. Sullivan, *et al.*, "Metabolic Regulation as a Control for Lipid Disorders. II. Influence of (–)-Hydroxycitrate on Genetically and Experimentally Induced Hypertriglyceridemia in the Rat," *The American Journal of Clinical Nutrition* 30, 5 (May 1977) 777–784.
14. Lowenstein, 1970, who provides the basis for Figure 3, concludes that in the rat the citrate pathway is by far the most significant. However, for humans this pathway is known to be less (how much less?) active. See here: G. E. Hoffmann, H. Andres, L. Weiss, C. Kreisel and R. Sander, "Lipogenesis in Man: Properties and Organ Distribution of ATP Citrate (*pro*-3S)-Lyase," *Biochimica et Biophysica Acta* 620 (1980) 151–158; also see A. Sener and W. J. Malaisse, "Hexose Metabolism in Pancreatic Islets. Effect of (–)-Hydroxycitrate upon Fatty Acid Synthesis and Insulin Release in Glucose-Stimulated Islets," *Biochimie* 73 (1991) 1287–1290; Hoja Chee, Dale R. Romsos and Gilbert A. Leveille, "Influence of (–)-Hydroxycitrate on Lipogenesis in Chickens and Rats," *Journal of Nutrition* 107, 1 (1977) 112–119. The latest research paper on this topic available to the authors is by Ying Zhang, Kamlesh C. Agarwal, *et al.*, "Nonhomogeneous Labeling of Liver Extra-mitochondrial Acetyl-CoA," *The Journal of Biological Chemistry* 268 (1994, in press).
15. See the discussions of these points in Donald Voet and Judith G. Voet, *Biochemistry* (New York: John Wiley & Sons, 1990); and in Arthur C. Guyton, *Textbook of Medical Physiology*, eighth edition (Philadelphia: W. B. Saunders Company, 1991) Chapter 67.
16. Lowenstein and Brunengraber, 1981, 496–497; Surinder Cheema-Dhadli, Mitchell L. Halperin and Clifford C. Leznoff, "Inhibition of Enzymes which Interact with Citrate by (–)-Hydroxycitrate and 1,2,3,-Tricarboxybenzene," *European Journal of Biochemistry* 38 (1973) 98–102.

Experimental proof that acetoacetate can act in a compensatory manner is given in Melvin M. Mathias, Ann C. Sullivan and James G. Hamilton, "Fatty Acid and Cholesterol Synthesis from Specifically Labeled Leucine by Isolated Rat Hepatocytes," *Lipids* 16, 10 (1981) 739–743. On yet other possible responses to a decrease in substrate supply, see Clive R. Pullinger and Geoffrey F. Gibbons, "The Role of Substrate Supply in the Regulation of Cholesterol Biosynthesis in Rat Hepatocytes," *Biochem. J.* 210 (1983) 625–632.

17. Theo A. Berkhout, *et al.*, "The Effect of (–)-Hydroxycitrate on the Activity of the Low-Density-Lipoprotein Receptor and 3-hydroxy-3-methylglutaryl-CoA Reductase Levels in the Human Hepatoma Cell Line Hep G2," *Biochem. J.* 272 (1990) 181–186.
18. Berkhout, *et al.*, 1990; Brunengraber, *et al.*, 1972.
19. *Journal of Biological Chemistry*, 1971.
20. Brunengraber, *et al.*, 1972; C. Barth, J. Hackenschmidt, H. Ullmann and K. Decker, "Inhibition of Cholesterol Synthesis by (–)-Hydroxycitrate in Perfused Rat Liver. Evidence for an Extramitochondrial Mevalonate Synthesis from Acetyl Coenzyme A," *Febs Letters* 22, 3 (May 1972) 343–346.
21. Sullivan, *et al.*, 1972.
22. Ann C. Sullivan, Joseph Triscari, James G. Hamilton, O. Neal Miller and Victor R. Wheatley, "Effect of (–)-Hydroxycitrate upon the Accumulation of Lipid in the Rat: I. Lipogenesis," *Lipids* 9 (1974) 121–128.
23. "Metabolic regulation as a control for lipid disorders. II. Influence of (–)-Hydroxycitrate on Genetically and Experimentally Induced Hypertriglyceridemia in the Rat," *The American Journal of Clinical Nutrition* 30, 5 (May 1977) 777–784.
24. Ibid.; Sullivan, Triscari, and Hamilton, "Hypolipidemic Activity of (–)-Hydroxycitrate," *Lipids* 12, 1 (1977) 1–9; Triscari and Sullivan, "Comparative Effects of (–)-Hydroxycitrate and (+)-allo-Hydroxycitrate on Acetyl CoA Carboxylase and Fatty Acid and Cholesterol Synthesis *in vivo*," *Lipids* 12, 4 (April 1977) 357–363.
25. Brunengraber, *et al.*, 1972; Barth, *et al.*, 1972
26. Hoja Chee, Dale R. Romsos and Gilbert A. Leveille, "Influence of (–)-Hydroxycitrate on Lipogenesis in Chickens and Rats," *Journal of Nutrition* 107, 1 (1977) 112–119.
27. See remarks in *Lipids* 12, 4 (1977) 362, note 46.
28. Geoffrey F. Gibbons, Christopher P. Attwell Thomas and Clive R. Pullinger, "The Metabolic Route by which Oleate is Converted into Cholesterol in Rat Hepatocytes," *Biochem. J.* 235 (1986) 19–24.
29. Charles R. Bowden, Kevin D. White and Gene F. Tutwiler, "Energy Intake of Cafeteria-Diet and Chow-Fed Rats in Response to Amphetamine, Fenfluramine, (–)-Hydroxycitrate, and Naloxone," *The Journal of Obesity and Weight Regulation* 4, 1 (Spring 1985) 5–13.
30. Berkhout, *et al.*, 1990.
31. Anthony A. Conte, "A Non-Prescription Alternative in Weight Reduction Therapy," *The Bariatrician* (Summer 1993) 17–19.

32. Ann C. Sullivan, Joseph Triscari and Karen Comai, "Pharmacological Modulation of Lipid Metabolism for the Treatment of Obesity," *International Journal of Obesity*, 8, Suppl. 1 (1984) 241–248.

33. Sullivan, Triscari, *et al.*, "Effect of (–)-Hydroxycitrate upon the Accumulation of Lipid in the Rat: II. Appetite," *Lipids* 9 (1974) 129–134.

34. Gloria R. Leon, "A Behavioral Approach to Obesity," *The American Journal of Clinical Nutrition* 30 (May 1977) 785–789.

35. Jaak Panksepp, Alan Pollack, Rick B. Meeker and Ann C. Sullivan, "(–)-Hydroxycitrate and Conditioned Aversions," *Pharmacology Biochemistry & Behavior*, 6 (1977) 683–687.

36. A. C. Sullivan and J. Triscari, "Metabolic Regulation as a Control for Lipid Disorders. I. Influence of (–)-Hydroxycitrate on Experimentally-Induced Obesity in the Rodent," *The American Journal of Clinical Nutrition* 30, 5 (1977) 767–776.

37. Sullivan, *et al.*, ". . . II. Appetite," *Lipids*, 1974.

38. See note 36.

39. A. C. Sullivan, *et al.*, "Metabolic Inhibitors of Lipid Biosynthesis as Anti-obesity Agents," in P. B. Curtis-Prior, ed., *Biochemical Pharmacology of Obesity* (Amsterdam: Elsevier Science Publishers, 1983) 311–325.

40. A. C. Sullivan, *et al.*, "The Influence of (–)-Hydroxycitrate on *in vivo* Rates of Hepatic Glycogenesis, Lipogenesis and Cholesterogenesis," *Federation Proceedings* 33 (1974) 656; Sullivan and Triscari, "Possible Interrelationship Between Metabolic Flux and Appetite," in D. Novin, W. Wyriwicka and G. Bray, eds., *Hunger: Basic Mechanisms and Clinical Implications* (New York: Raven Press, 1976) 115–125; Ann C. Sullivan and Rhoda K. Gruen, "Mechanisms of Appetite Modulation by Drugs," *Federation Proceedings* 44, 1, Part I (1985) 139–144.

41. K. J. Acheson, *et al.*, *The Amer. Journal of Clinical Nutrition* 48 (1988) 240*ff.*

42. R. L. Leibel in P. D. Bray and V. S. Marcum, eds., *Human Nutrition: Clinical and Biomedical Aspects* (1980) 239.

43. See note 39; also G. Harvey Anderson, "Regulation of Food Intake," Chapter 35 in Maurice E. Shils, James A. Olson and Moshe Shike, eds., *Modern Nutrition in Health and Disease*, 8th edition (Philadelphia: Lea & Febiger, 1994) 524–536.

44. R. C. Bonadonna and R. A. Defronzo, "Glucose Metabolism in Obesity and Type II Diabetes," in Per Björntorp and Bernard N. Brodoff, eds., *Obesity* (Philadelphia: J. B. Lippincott Company, 1992) 474–501.

45. F. Nomura, K. Chinishi, *et al.*, "Liver Function in Moderate Obesity—Study in 534 Moderately Obese Subjects Among 4,613 Male Company Employees," *International Journal of Obesity* 10 (1986) 349–354.

46. See notes 26–28.

47. See Mark McCarty, note 2.

48. Barry E. Levin, Joseph Triscari and Ann C. Sullivan, "Altered Sympathetic Activity During Development of Diet-Induced Obesity in Rat," *American Journal of Physiology* 244, 2 (1983) R347–R355; E. Bonora,

C. Coscelli and U. Butturini, "Relationship Between Insulin Resistance, Insulin Secretion and Insulin Metabolism in Simple Obesity," *International Journal of Obesity* 9 (1985) 307–312.

49. M. E. Lean, "Evidence for Brown Adipose Tissue in Humans," in Per Björntorp and Bernard N. Brodoff, eds., *Obesity* (Philadelphia: J. B. Lippincott Company, 1992) 117–129.
50. See the appropriate section in Chapter 2 of Dallas Clouatre, *Anti-Fat Nutrients*, second edition (San Francisco: PAX Publishing, 1993).
51. Steen Jaedig and Nels C. Henningsen, "Increased Metabolic Rate in Obese Women After Ingestion of Potassium, Magnesium- and Phosphate-enriched Orange Juice or Injection of Ephedrine," *International Journal of Obesity* 15 (1991) 429–436. These tests included phosphorous supplementation, but it is arguable that the American diet already contains too much phosphorous. Regarding the much disputed role of thermogenesis (or its lack) in the etiology of human weight gain, see Michael J. Stock, "Thermogenesis and Energy Balance," *International Journal of Obesity* 16, Suppl. 2 (1993) S13–S16.
52. Sullivan and Triscari, ". . . I. Influence of (–)-Hydroxycitrate . . . Obesity in the Rodent," 1977, p. 773.
53. M. R. C. Greenwood, M. P. Cleary, R. Gruen, D. Blase, J. S. Stern, J. Triscari and A. C. Sullivan, "Effect of (–)-Hydroxycitrate on Development of Obesity in the Zucker Obese Rat," *American Journal of Physiology* 240 (1981) E72–E78.
54. B. A. Scoville, "Review of Amphetamine-like Drugs by the Food and Drug Administration: Clinical Data and Value Judgements," in *Obesity in Perspective: Proceedings of the Fogarty Conference* (U.S. Government Printing Office, 1973) 441–443; A. C. Sullivan and K. Comai, "Pharmacological Treatment of Obesity," *International Journal of Obesity* 2 (1978) 167–189; Trevor Silverstone, "Drugs, Appetite and Obesity: A Personal Odyssey," *International Journal of Obesity* 16, Suppl. 2 (1992) S49–S52; a less technical general review of many natural agents can be found in D. Clouatre, *Anti-Fat Nutrients.*
55. A. C. Sullivan, J. Triscari and L. Cheng, "Appetite Regulation by Drugs and Endogenous Substances," Chapter 10 in Myron Winick, ed., *Nutrition and Drugs* (New York: Wiley & Sons, 1983) 139–167.
56. Jules Hirsch and Rudolph L. Leibel, "Clinical Review 28: A Biological Basis for Human Obesity," *Journal of Clinical Endocrinology and Metabolism* 73, 6 (1991) 1153–1157.
57. Sullivan, Hamilton, Miller and Wheatly, *Archives of Biochemistry and Biophysics*, 1972.
58. Chema-Dhadli, *et al.*, 1973.
59. Lowenstein and Brunengraber, 1981.
60. See D. Clouatre, *Anti-Fat Nutrients.*
61. See Matthias Rath, *Eradicating Heart Disease* (San Francisco: Health Now, 1993); Linus Pauling likewise has long championed the use of vitamin C for these purposes.